Knowledge and Reasoning for Answering Questions 2009

(KRAQ 2009)

AA005711

Held at ACL-IJCNLP 2009

Singapore
6 August 2009

ISBN: 978-1-61738-448-6

Printed from e-media with permission by:

Curran Associates, Inc.
57 Morehouse Lane
Red Hook, NY 12571

CURRAN ASSOCIATES INC.
proceedings
.com

Some format issues inherent in the e-media version may also appear in this print version.

Printed by Curran Associates, Inc. (2010)

Association for Computational Linguistics
209 N. Eighth Street
Stroudsburg, Pennsylvania 18360

Phone: 1-570-476-8006
Fax: 1-570-476-0860

acl@aclweb.org

Additional copies of this publication are available from:

Curran Associates, Inc.
57 Morehouse Lane
Red Hook, NY 12571 USA
Phone: 845-758-0400
Fax: 845-758-2634
Email: curran@proceedings.com
Web: www.proceedings.com

Foreword

The introduction of reasoning capabilities in question-answering (QA) systems appeared in the late 70s. A second generation of QA systems, aimed at being cooperative, emerged in the late 80s - early 90s. In these systems, quite advanced reasoning models were developed on closed domains to go beyond the production of direct responses to a query, in particular when the query has no response or when it contains misconceptions. More recently, systems such as JAVELIN, Inference WEB or Cogex, operating over open domains, gradually integrated inferential components, but not as advanced as those of the 90s. Performances of these systems in the recent TREC-QA tracks show that reasoning components substantially improve the response relevance and accuracy. They can also potentially be much more cooperative. However, there is still a long way before being able to produce accurate, cooperative and robust QA systems, because of the very large complexity of natural systems and of the need to make several communities work together on common grounds.

Recent foundational, methodological and technological developments in knowledge representation (e.g. ontologies, knowledge bases incorporating various forms of incompleteness or uncertainty), in advanced reasoning forms (e.g. data fusion-integration, argumentation, decision theory, fuzzy logic, incomplete knowledge bases, etc.), in advanced language processing resources and techniques (for question processing as well as for generating responses) including semantic role labelling and the recognition and resolution of temporal and spatial expressions, and recent progress in HLT and formal pragmatics (user models, intentions, etc.) make it possible to foresee the elaboration of much more accurate, cooperative and robust systems dedicated to answering questions from multimedia supports or from textual data, from e.g. online texts or web pages, operating either on open or closed domains. The user interface aspects (input, output (e.g. SMS or advanced interfaces), on line help, dialogue, etc.) are also crucial for the viability of such systems.

We thanks very much the Programme Committee for producing accurate reviews.

Patrick Saint-Dizier and Marie-Francine Moens (Co-chairs).

Organizers

Co-chairs:

Patrick Saint-Dizier, stdizier@irit.fr
Marie-Francine Moens, Marie-Francine.Moens@cs.kuleuven.be

Program Committee:

Sivaji Bandyopadhyay (India)
Johan Bos (Italy)
Gosse Bouma (The Netherlands)
Brigitte Grau (France)
Kentaro Inui (Japan)
Asanee Kawtrakul (Thailand)
Jochen Leidner (USA)
Sien Moens (Belgium)
Matteo Negri (Italy)
Silvia Quarteroni (Italy)
Alan Ramsay (UK)
Patrick Saint-Dizier (France)
Tomek Strzalkowski (USA)
Michael Wiegand (Germany)

Table of Contents

Conference Program

Thursday, 6 August 2009

13:50–14:00 Welcome Address

14:00–15:00 Invited Talk, Pierre Zweigenbaum
Knowledge and Reasoning for Medical Question-Answering

14:00–15:00 *Knowledge and Reasoning for Medical Question-Answering*
Pierre Zweigenbaum

15:00–15:30 *The Development of a Question-Answering Services System for the Farmer through SMS: Query Analysis*
Mukda Suktarachan, Patthrawan Rattanamanee and Asanee Kawtrakul

15:30–16:00 Coffee Break, Level 3, Suntec

16:00–16:20 *QAST: Question Answering System for ThaiWikipedia*
Wittawat Jitkrittum, Choochart Haruechaiyasak and Thanaruk Theeramunkong

16:20–16:40 *Some Challenges in the Design of Comparative and Evaluative Question Answering Systems*
Nathalie Lim, Patrick Saint-Dizier and Rachel Roxas

16:40–17:00 *Addressing How-to Questions using a Spoken Dialogue System: a Viable Approach?*
Silvia Quarteroni and Patrick Saint-Dizier

17:00–17:30 Invited Talk, Manfred Stede
Question Answering: Reasoning, Mining, or Crowdsourcing?

Knowledge and Reasoning for Medical Question-Answering

Pierre Zweigenbaum
CNRS, LIMSI
Orsay, F-91403 France
pz@limsi.fr

Abstract

Restricted domains such as medicine set a context where question-answering is more likely expected to be associated with knowledge and reasoning (Mollá and Vicedo, 2007; Ferret and Zweigenbaum, 2007). On the one hand, knowledge and reasoning may be more necessary than in open-domain question-answering because of more specific or more difficult questions. On the other hand, it may also be more manageable, since by definition restricted-domain QA should not have to face the same breadth of questions as open-domain QA. It is therefore interesting to study the role of knowledge and reasoning in restricted-domain question-answering systems. We shall do so in the case of the (bio-)medical domain, which has a long tradition of investigating knowledge representation and reasoning and, more generally, artificial intelligence methods (Shortliffe et al., 1975), and which has seen a growing interest in question-answering systems (Zweigenbaum, 2003; Yu et al., 2005; Demner-Fushman and Lin, 2007; Zweigenbaum et al., 2007).

1 Knowledge and Reasoning for Processing Medical Questions

Medical question-answering has to address questions other than the usual factual questions of most QA evaluations. This calls for different question classifications (Ely et al., 2000; Yu et al., 2005), especially to determine whether a given question can be answered using medical knowledge backed with a sufficient level of evidence (Lin and Demner-Fushman, 2005; Kilicoglu et al., 2009). This can also lead to a different representation of questions, for instance using a structured representation such as PICO (Niu et al., 2003; Huang et al., 2006; Demner-Fushman and Lin, 2007) or simple concepts and relations (Lin, 2001; Jacquemart and Zweigenbaum, 2003).

2 Knowledge and Reasoning for Finding Medical Answers

Answers to medical questions should be searched in the most reliable data available. When data exist in structured knowledge bases (*e.g.* a drug compendium), it may be more appropriate to query such knowledge bases directly. Therefore an approach akin to that of Start/Omnibase (Lin and Katz, 2003) may be indicated. When answers are to be found in a collection of documents, as is the case in traditional question-answering systems, a representation of the information contained in these documents can be built, offline (Fleischman et al., 2003; Sang et al., 2005; Delbecque et al., 2005) or dynamically.

In medical QA systems, both document analysis and question analysis nearly always rely on extensive knowledge of domain concepts and relations, *e.g.* as provided by the UMLS knowledge sources (McCray and Nelson, 1995). More than named entities, systems need to detect mentions of concepts (Aronson, 2001) and their relations (Rindflesch et al., 2005). Besides, taking into account the structure of documents such as scientific articles or encyclopedia entries may help focus on more relevant sections (Niu and Hirst, 2004; Sang et al., 2005). Finally, answers to complex medical questions often need to span more than one sentence. Extractive summarization is performed both from single documents (Demner-Fushman and Lin, 2007) and from multiple documents (Fiszman et al., 2008).

Proceedings of the 2009 Workshop on Knowledge and Reasoning for Answering Questions, ACL-IJCNLP 2009, pages 1–2,
Suntec, Singapore, 6 August 2009.

References

Alan R. Aronson. 2001. Effective mapping of biomedical text to the UMLS Metathesaurus: The MetaMap program. *Journal of the American Medical Informatics Association*, 8(suppl):17–21.

Thierry Delbecque, Pierre Jacquemart, and Pierre Zweigenbaum. 2005. Indexing UMLS semantic types for medical question-answering. In Rolf Engelbrecht, Antoine Geissbuhler, Christian Lovis, and G. Mihalas, editors, *Proceedings Medical Informatics Europe*, volume 116 of *Studies in Health Technology and Informatics*, pages 805–810, Amsterdam. IOS Press.

Dina Demner-Fushman and Jimmy Lin. 2007. Answering clinical questions with knowledge-based and statistical techniques. *Computational Linguistics*, 33(1):63–103.

John W. Ely, Jerome A. Osheroff, Paul N. Gorman, Mark H. Ebell, M. Lee Chambliss, Eric A. Pifer, and P. Zoe Stavri. 2000. A taxonomy of generic clinical questions: classification study. *BMJ*, 321:429–432. Available at `http://bmj.com/cgi/content/full/321/7258/429`.

Olivier Ferret and Pierre Zweigenbaum. 2007. Représentation des connaissances pour les systèmes de question-réponse. In Brigitte Grau and Jean-Pierre Chevallet, editors, *La recherche d'informations précises : traitement automatique de la langue, apprentissage et connaissances pour les systèmes de question-réponse*, chapter 4, pages 133–169. Hermès-Lavoisier, Paris.

Marcelo Fiszman, Dina Demner-Fushman, Halil Kilicoglu, and Thomas C Rindflesch. 2008. Automatic summarization of MEDLINE citations for evidence-based medical treatment: A topic-oriented evaluation. *J Biomed Inform*, November.

Michael Fleischman, Abdessamad Echihabi, and Eduard Hovy. 2003. Offline strategies for online question answering: Answering questions before they are asked. In *Proceedings of the ACL Conference*, pages 1–7, Sapporo, Japan.

Xiaoli Huang, Jimmy Lin, and Dina Demner-Fushman. 2006. Evaluation of PICO as a knowledge representation for clinical questions. In *AMIA Annu Symp Proc*, page 359–63.

Pierre Jacquemart and Pierre Zweigenbaum. 2003. Towards a medical question-answering system: a feasibility study. In Robert Baud, Marius Fieschi, Pierre Le Beux, and Patrick Ruch, editors, *Proceedings Medical Informatics Europe*, volume 95 of *Studies in Health Technology and Informatics*, pages 463–468, Amsterdam. IOS Press.

Halil Kilicoglu, Dina Demner-Fushman, Thomas C Rindflesch, Nancy L Wilczynski, and R Brian Haynes. 2009. Towards automatic recognition of scientifically rigorous clinical research evidence. *J Am Med Inform Assoc*, 16(1):25–31.

Jimmy Lin and Dina Demner-Fushman. 2005. "Bag of words" is not enough for strength of evidence classification. In *AMIA Annu Symp Proc*, page 1031.

Jimmy Lin and Boris Katz. 2003. Question answering techniques for the World Wide Web. In *Tutorial at EACL 2003*, Budapest. ACL.

Jimmy Lin. 2001. Indexing and retrieving natural language using ternary expressions. Master's thesis, Massachusetts Institute of Technology.

Alexa T. McCray and Stuart J. Nelson. 1995. The semantics of the UMLS knowledge sources. *Methods of Information in Medicine*, 34(1/2).

Diego Mollá and José Luis Vicedo. 2007. Question answering in restricted domains: An overview. *Computational Linguistics*, 33(1):41–61.

Yun Niu and Graeme Hirst. 2004. Analysis of semantic classes in medical text for question answering. In *Proceedings ACL 2004 Workshop on Question Answering in Restricted Domains*. ACL.

Yun Niu, Graeme Hirst, Gregory McArthur, and Patricia Rodriguez-Gianolli. 2003. Answering clinical questions with role identification. In *ACL Workshop Natural Language Processing in Biomedicine*, pages 73–80. ACL.

Thomas C. Rindflesch, Marcelo Fiszman, and B. Libbus. 2005. Semantic interpretation for the biomedical literature. In H Chen, S Fuller, WR Hersh, and C Friedman, editors, *Medical informatics: Advances in knowledge management and data mining in biomedicine*, pages 399–422, Berlin / Heidelberg. Springer.

Erik Tjong Kim Sang, Gosse Bouma, and Maarten de Rijke. 2005. Developing offline strategies for answering medical questions. In *Proceedings AAAI-05 workshop on Question Answering in restricted domains*, pages 41–45. AAAI.

E H Shortliffe, R Davis, S G Axline, B G Buchanan, C C Green, and S N Cohen. 1975. Computer-based consultations in clinical therapeutics: explanation and rule acquisition capabilities of the MYCIN system. *Comput Biomed Res*, 8(4):303–20, August.

Hong Yu, Carl Sable, and Hai Ran Zhu. 2005. Classifying medical questions based on an evidence taxonomy. In *Proceedings AAAI 2005 Workshop on Question Answering in Restricted Domains*. AAAI.

Pierre Zweigenbaum, Dina Demner-Fushman, Hong Yu, and K. Bretonnel Cohen. 2007. Frontiers of biomedical text mining: current progress. *Briefings in Bioinformatics*, 8:358–375, October. doi:10.1093/bib/bbm045.

Pierre Zweigenbaum. 2003. Question answering in biomedicine. In Maarten de Rijke and Bonnie Webber, editors, *Proceedings Workshop on Natural Language Processing for Question Answering, EACL 2003*, pages 1–4, Budapest. ACL. Keynote speech.

The Development of a Question-Answering Services System for the Farmer through SMS: Query Analysis

Mukda Suktarachan,
Patthrawan Rattanamanee
Department of Computer Engineering, Kasetsart University, Bangkok, Thailand, 10900
naist_da_da@yahoo.com,
tiptop317@hotmail.com

Asanee Kawtrakul
Department of Computer Engineering, Kasetsart University, Bangkok, Thailand, 10900
National Electronics and Computer Technology Center, Thailand
asanee_naist@yahoo.com
asanee.kawtrakul@nectec.or.th

Abstract

In this paper, we propose the development of the Question-Answering Services System for the Farmer, through SMS, by focusing on query analysis and annotation based on a similar technique previously applied to language generation, thematic roles, and primitive systems of the Lexical Conceptual Structure (LCS). The annotation places emphasis on the semantics model of "What" and "How" queries, lexical inference identification, and semantic role, for the answer. Finally, we show how these annotations and inference rules contribute to the generalization of the matching system over semantic categories in order to have a large scale question-answering system.

1 Challenges and Goals

In the era of Information and Communications Technology (ICT), mobile is a fast and convenient way to communicate over a network. Knowledge service via a mobile as "a right information for a right man" is a challenging task. However, this means of interchange between persons has the limitation of personal timing. Therefore, Short Message Service (SMS) is a better way for giving knowledge service, especially automatic interchange of short text messages, by providing the information from an automatic Question & Answering System.

From the results of the statistical ICT data survey concerning the number and percent of the population 6 years of age and over who use information and communication technology: 2003 - 2007 by the National Statistical Office[1], Thailand, it was found that 47.2% of people in the entire kingdom have owned their mobile(s). Consequently, communicating via SMS facilitates an effective knowledge service for supporting the farmers in problem-solving, decision making, and early warning, and also supports the government, or a related organization, in order to e-communicate to the farmer by changing the model of "Training and Visit" to e-service and changing the collective to support cooperative problem solving. This kind of communication will provide the necessary long-term cost reductions to the agricultural economy in the areas of travel, visiting, productivity, etc.

Nowadays, providing a knowledge service through SMS is not limited to only a Question-Answering Services System, but also for such one-way services as early warning systems, for example, a Tsunami Alert System[2], a FloodSMS – Early Detection and Warning of Catastrophic Flooding via SMS[3], etc.

The development of a Question-Answering Services System through SMS is not the design of a new technology. There have been several theories developed earlier, in the context of NLP or cognitive sciences, such as Natural Language Information Retrieval (NLIR), rule based Q&A, etc. Nevertheless, some former theories of Q&A relied on complex semantic information. For instance, a Wireless Natural Language Search Engine [6] was implemented using a system resid-

[1] http://web.nso.go.th/en/survey/keystat/keystat08.pdf
[2] http://www.wap.ait.ac.th/tsunami.html
[3] http://www.netsquared.org/projects/floodsms-%E2%80%93-early-detection-and-warning-catastrophic-flooding-sms

Proceedings of the 2009 Workshop on Knowledge and Reasoning for Answering Questions, ACL-IJCNLP 2009, pages 3–10, Suntec, Singapore, 6 August 2009.

ing on a server, which can translate questions or phrases into search engine queries or queries to SOAP Web services, where a gateway mediates between the mobile network and the Internet. Also, [15] developed the SMS for Question-Answering in the m-Learning Scenario System by using the Simple Matching Algorithm to match the learners' answer messages with the original answer string, thus facilitating the learners to get the necessary feedback and assessment.

In this paper, we propose the development of the Question-Answering Services System for the Farmer through SMS by focusing on query analysis and annotation, as well as on selected text matching utilizing lexical inference and semantic roles. The annotation emphasizes the semantics model of "What" and "How" queries. Finally, we show how these annotations and inference rules contribute to the generalization of the matching system over semantic categories in order to have a large scale question-answering system.

In the current stage, we have designed Q&A schema with thematic roles and have borrowed some primitive systems of the Lexical Conceptual Structure (LCS). Also, we are annotating 1000 questions and text related to the query (but we randomly choose 100 pairs of Q&A for the experiment). In the same time, we are generalizing inference rules in order to match a question to its answer. This is particularly crucial when there is no straightforward response, e.g. when they require some form of lexical inference, elaboration, and reasoning or when the response is not a simple item, but a well-formed fragment of text, e.g. a chain of events leading to a consequence, a procedure, etc.

The project we present here emerged from a need of the real end-users, the Agricultural Land Reform Office, Ministry of Agriculture and Cooperative, Thailand, in the project of ALRO CyberBrain [3], which is a social network framework that combines approaches based on knowledge science and engineering with language engineering, consisting of an ontology-based search engine, information extraction for Q&A system, knowledge aggregation through a knowledge portal and visualized in a browser with semantic links between problems, methods of problems solving and man who is the problem solver (PMM map Model) [1]. The main goal is to develop tools for e-Farming, in particular rice farming, so that farmers can easily get information on farming rice and rice diseases. Now, it has been extended to provide question-answering services for the farmers through SMS [2].

2 Problem Statements

There are two main problems in Q&A analysis: semantic interpretation for a question word and answer identification.

2.1 Question's Semantic Roles

2.1.1 Question Word Interpretation.

In general, when we query for the answer by a traditional search engine system, we might get many answers at different levels, depending on the role of the question: Definition vs Fact or set of Facts. For example, with the question

Q1: "โรค|ไหม้|คือ|อะไร"

Rice| Blast| is| what

"What is a Rice Blast?"

The answer can be returned as the definitions, fact or a set of facts, which are:

A1.1: Blast, also called rotten neck, is one of the most destructive diseases of Missouri rice. Blast does not develop every year but is very destructive when it occurs.[4]

A1.2: Disease of Leave Burnt caused by Pyricularia Oryzae can destroy all rice growing period from start until harvest period.[5]

The answer can be returned as the characteristics detail or set of facts, such as the following:

A1.3 : Blast symptoms can occur on leaves, leaf collars, nodes and panicles. Leaf spots are typically diamond shaped, with gray- white centers and brown to red-brown margins. Fully developed leaf lesions are approximately 0.4 to 0.7 inch long and 0.1 to 0.2 inch wide. Both the shape and color vary depending on the environment, age of the lesion and rice variety.[6]

2.1.2 Variety of Question Forms.

In natural language, the question can be asked with different words and styles, for example:

Q2.1:ลักษณะ|การระบาด|ของ|โรค|ไหม้|เป็น|อย่างไร

situation| outbreak| of| disease| Rice Blast| is| how

"What is the situation of Rice Blast?"

Q2.2:การระบาด|ของ|โรค|ไหม้|มี|ลักษณะ|อย่างไร

outbreak| of| disease| Rice Blast| is| characteristic| how

"How does the rice blast outbreak look like?"

4 http://aes.missouri.edu/delta/muguide/mp645.stm

5 http://www.sotus.co.th/article_4.html

6 http://aes.missouri.edu/delta/muguide/mp645.stm

Q2.3:โรค|ไหม้|ระบาด|ได้|อย่างไร

Rice Blast| disperse| able| how

"How can the rice blast disperse?"

The reply can be returned the same answers with a descriptive set of events, as the following:

A2.1: *To prevent the Rice Blast: for the places that we often found the disease, use the disease-resistant rice variety. Don't sow the rice seed too densely. Don't use to much Nitrogen. If it is severe outbreak and it is the state of young plant, plow and sow again. If it was the epidemic state, use Fungus-Removal chemical as Carbendasim.*

A2.2: *Brown spot may be reduced by balanced fertilization, crop rotation, and the use of high quality planting seed. Seed treatment fungicides reduce the incidence and severity of seedling blight caused by this fungus.*

The examples above show that using different verbs or noun phrases can be represent the same meaning. Moreover, there is non-correspondent focus word between Q and A.

2.2 Answer Type Identification

2.2.1 Ambiguity between subtopic and answer form

To identify the answer, sometimes there is an ambiguity that verb phrases occurring after the focus word of the question can be both subtopics and the answer, like a procedural answer, for example,:

Q3: วิธีการ|ป้องกัน|โรค|ไหม้|ทำ|ได้|อย่างไร

method| control| Rice Blast| to do| how

"What method can be used to control Rice Blast?"

A3: วิธีการ|ป้องกัน|โรค|ไหม้|มี|ดังนี้

method| control| Rice Blast| have| such as

"Methods for preventing the Rice Blast are:"

- ใช้|สารเคมี|ที่|เหมาะสม
  use| Chemical Substance | that| appropriate
  "Use appropriate Chemical Substance."
- ใช้|พันธุ์|ที่|เหมาะสม
  use| type of rice | that| appropriate
  "Use appropriate type of rice."
- ใช้|กลไก|ใน|การ|ป้องกัน
  use| mechanism| in| prevent
  "Use mechanism to prevent."
- ใช้|วิธีการ|ผสมผสาน
  use| methods| hybrid
  "Use hybrid methods."

The examples above convey the 4 types of method for Rice Blast control or names of methods, but it is not the process or the answers that represent how to control the disease.

2.2.2 Non-correspondence between Q & A:

Sometimes, the question and answer were not matched because the clue words or focus words in the question have never appeared in the answers. This makes the question not correspond to the answer and also causes difficulty in finding the expected answer. For example,

Q4: สามารถ|ควบคุม|แมลง|ศัตรู|ข้าว|เหล่านี้|ได้|อย่างไร

can| control| pests | rice | these | How

"How can these rice pests be controlled?"

A4: แมลง|ศัตรู|เหล่านี้|สามารถ|กำจัด|ได้|โดย|ใช้|วิธีการ|หลาย|ประการ|รวม|กัน| |คือ| |ปลูก|ข้าว|พันธุ์|ต้านทาน|โรค|,| |ปลูก|ข้าว|ตาม|ฤดูกาล|, |ควบคุม|ระดับ|น้ำ|ใน|นา |และ|ไม่|ควร|ใช้|สาร|ฆ่า|แมลง|ที่|ทำ|ให้|เกิด|การ|เพิ่ม|ระบาด||ของ|โรค|

"These pests can be managed through integrated approach including sowing insect resistant rice varieties, sowing rice crop at recommended time, proper water management conservation and augmentation of bio-control predators."

From the example, the focus word of the question is "control," but there is no word "control" in the answer. For this kind of Q&A matching solution, WordNet and ontology are necessary.

3 Outline of the Project and Methodology

The needs of the Thai Ministry of Agriculture have been specified in a simple way via a corpus composed of (1) questions raised in real life by farmers (about 1000 questions), (2) the responses which have been provided by experts, based on existing documents (possibly several responses per question) and, quite often, (3) the texts they originate from. In general, the response is found in a unique text: there are no multiple answers, since most texts are not redundant, although some responses, in particular complex (e.g. evaluative questions) or indirect ones, may involve the taking into account of several independent texts. We will not address here the problem of message length reduction so that it fits into an SMS format (although this is also an important semantic problem).

The system overview is shown in Figure 2.

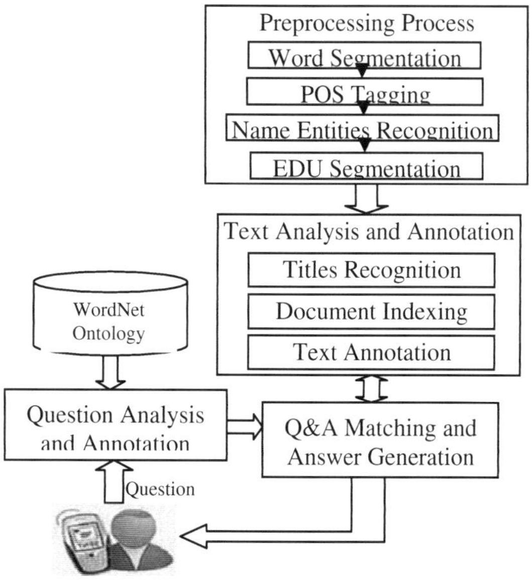

Figure 2. System Architecture

To develop a Thai QA system, the preprocessing of Thai morphology and syntax is necessary. The NAIST lab at the University of Kasetsart has basic tools to manage morphological analysis, parts-of-speech recognition, simple syntactic analysis, as well as Thai parsing, and an Element Discourse Unit System (EDU). These tools were designed as basic tools in natural language processing applications. (accessible on http://vivaldi.cpe.ku.ac.th:9292/ with a recommendation to use the Mozilla Firefox browser)

A few examples of question-answer pairs are:

Q5: วิธีการ|ป้องกัน|กำจัด|ข้าว|วัชพืช|ทำ|ได้|อย่างไร

"How to prevent the Weedy rice"

A5.1: ควร|เว้น|ปลูก|ข้าว|บาง|ฤดู

"Skip some seasons when growing rice,"

A5.2: ปลูก|พืช|อายุ|สั้น|อื่น

"Grow hydrotonics plants."

Q6: โรค|ใบ|ขีด|โปร่ง|แสง|มี|วิธีการ|ควบคุม|อย่างไร

"How to control the Bacterial Leaf Streak Disease"

A6: *ไม่|ควร|ใส่|ปุ๋ย|ไนโตรเจน|มาก|เกินไป|*

"Do not put too much Nitrogen."

Q7: *ถ้า|พบ|เพลี้ย|ไฟ|ระบาด| |สามารถ|กำจัด|ด้วย|สาร|ฆ่า|แมลง|ชนิด|ใด*

"How to eradicate the rice thrips"

A7: *ฉีด|พ่น|ด้วย|มาลาไทออน|หรือ|คาร์บาริล|ทุก|อาทิตย์| |ใส่|ปุ๋ย|และ|ให้|น้ำ|ทุก| |ๆ| |สอง|วัน*

"Spray with Malathion or Carbaryl every week, add fertilizer and water every two days."

Questions are essentially factoid questions (e.g. best periods for rice planting, rice varieties suggestion, symptoms of a disease), why questions, where responses are chains of events (reasons for something to happen) and a large number of procedural questions [4], in particular for treating diseases. There are relatively few comparative or evaluative questions besides general questions, such as: What are the major rice pests?

In most cases, questions do not have responses which can be immediately found in the texts by standard term matching techniques. For example: *"How does the Sheath Blight affect the rice growth?"* has the following response in a text: *Plants heavily infected at these stages produce poorly filled grain, particularly in the lower portion of the panicle. Additional losses result from* ... Therefore, some lexical semantics devices (e.g. a semantic link between *affect* and *infect*) or more elaborated reasoning schemas, based on domain knowledge, are needed to allow appropriate question-text matching [11, 7]. The kind of domain knowledge at stake may be quite unexpected (i.e., not the main topics that everyone knows, but more subtle pieces of information, as will be seen in 4.3). This is the major challenge of this work, which we try to resolve via a full annotation of the matching process, from question parsing to response production, identifying matching and reasoning aspects.

Complex questions may, e.g., require the elaboration of a diagnosis from premises given in the question before finding the response, either factoid or procedural (*My rice has weedy leaves and some yellow spots, what should I do?*). This question requires one to select all texts where such a symptom is identified, and then, e.g., to enter into a dialogue with the user if there are several possible diagnoses, leading to different treatments.

The second aspect of this problem is to be able to extract the complete text portion that responds to the question. For that purpose we are developing an annotation methodology whose goal is to identify the different processes at stake and the needed resources. This method allows us to identify relevant text portions and then to delimit them appropriately.

4 The Question-Answering Process Annotation

Since the task is quite large (a large group of students are annotating a set of 600 questions and related texts), we need to establish norms and annotation guidelines. Using the research conducted at IRIT on annotating procedural questions and instructions based on semantic roles

(TextCoop project) and a few rhetorical relations (e.g. elaboration, example, explanation), we first annotated the questions and their corresponding responses in texts provided by the Thai Ministry of Agriculture. One of the challenges was to identify relevant linguistic marks or patterns [9, 10, 14].

There are many attempts to annotate arguments by means of primitives; our approach, here, is oriented towards the precise task at stake and the specific actions. Therefore roles are not as standard as they are in general. An earlier attempt with a similar technique applied to language generation was carried out in, e.g., [10, 7]. Semantic tags are either close to thematic roles (instrument, location, etc.) [8], or borrowed from the primitive systems of the Lexical Conceptual Structure (LCS) [13], in particular, to establish useful links between arguments or between a large variety of constituents, which thematic roles cannot do. For example, in *the first Thai university* we have a link between 'first' and 'Thai university' which is either loc_{temp} or $\text{loc}_{\text{+char+ident}}$, depending on the interpretation of *first* (oldest or the best). However, in a majority of cases, semantic roles based on thematic roles have a sufficient granularity, and these are the ones which are used in the examples in 4.1.

The main roles we consider are: agents (for humans and animals like insects, and metaphorically for diseases and natural forces), themes (undergoing actions, basically plants and soils, and artificial products), location (spatial), time (covering dates and also periods), instruments (from tools to chemical products), manners, means, conditions (under which to realize an action, or related to observation e.g. of a disease), cause, goals, and results.

Besides, the tags <action>…</action> or <fact>…</fact> were considered to tag the verb with it's arguments or adjuncts.

In the remainder of this section we briefly report the different steps of the process as they stand at the moment, i.e. almost at the end of the experimental stage, before automating knowledge acquisition, and implementing the application.

4.1 Dealing with Questions

As in most systems dealing with complex types of questions, questions are represented by a triple: the question type (which can be in our case polymorphic), the question focus (usually an NP or a VP in case events or procedures are induced) and the question body, annotated by means of semantic roles, as indicated above.

The main types of questions we have identified from our corpus are the following; they are quite different from standard classifications, but they correspond to more operational views:

- *F: fact,* with subtypes: temp (temporal, time, date), loc (location) or product,
- *E: an event* (with a subtype event: cause)
- *SF: set of facts*
- *SE: set of events* (not related, and without any form of sequence: different from SqE below)
- *PROC: procedure,* more or less complex, it may be just a single instruction; it can also describe the use of an instrument.
- *SqE: sequence of events,* which follow each other.
- *EVAL: evaluation,* making value decisions about issues or resolving controversies or differences of opinion.
- *DEF: definition,* the description of object.

Some questions may bear several non-conflicting types, in particular when the nature of the response is not straightforward to determine from the question. For example, *"What is the symptom of Bakanae?"* would get the types SF and SE.

An annotated question is, for example:

<question type=" SF or SE" focus=" symptom of *Bakanae*"> What <fact> is <theme> the symptom of *Bakanae* </theme> </fact> ? </question>

As can be noted, the response is the set of those facts that contribute, together or independently, to the spreading of the disease.

By the observation from 100 random interrogative sentences corpus analysis, we found that the semantic types of questions correspondent to the question words are the following

Q-Types	What	When	Where	Why	Who	Which	How
F	11	6	1		1	9	2
E				1			6
SF	3					15	3
SE	7					2	5
PROC							15
SqE							7
EVAL	2				1		
DEF	3						

Table 1 the correspondence between questions and semantic types of questions

From Table 1, it is clear that "what" and "how" questions vary in types of question, because they have many forms to use, for example, *"how + verb to be + noun", "how + do(es) + noun + verb", "how to", "how can", etc. or "what + verb to be + noun", "what + noun + auxiliary verb",* etc. This is why we point out the "What" and "How" questions.

4.2 Dealing with texts: document indexing and associated annotations

Texts are initially indexed based on the main terms they contain which are relevant w.r.t. the questions given in the corpus. Our representation resembles a frame approach, but it is more flexible since there is no predefined structure to represent indexes. This is more in accordance with the variety of texts in terms of contents. Indexes basically are formed from:

- Top-level terms that structure the domain: for example, concepts like symptom, spreading, treatment, time, place, effect, etc. where predicative (action terms) terms as well as entities are found,
- relatively generic terms, found in the questions and structured in the domain ontology: water, clean, control, eradicate, etc., which are organized w.r.t. the top concepts above,
- named entities, typed as: disease names, location names, chemical product names, bacteria names, etc.

In our representation, those generic terms (and near synonyms) are represented as predicates, while arguments are represented as attribute-value pairs (or attributes alone), include typed name entities and any kind of terms besides the generic terms.

Indexes are associated with texts in the text database. Indexes must remain general so that indexing is fast and as reliable as possible. The idea is that when a question is uttered, a small number of texts are first selected on the basis of the indexes for further analysis. An example below can be indexed and annotated [2] as the following:

Index: disease-name (Bakanae), symptoms (disease: Bakanae), origin (disease: Bakanae, place: California, date: 1999), spreading(disease: Bakanae, period: winter, medium: [soil, water]), treatment(disease: Bakanae, product).

<title type="goal" level="1" > Rice Bakanae </title>
<title type="goal" level="2">SYMPTOMS </title>
<task type = "SF">
<theme>Symptoms of Bakanae</theme> first appear about a month after planting. Infected seedlings appear to be taller, more slender, and slightly chlorotic ... The rapid elongation of infected plants is caused by the pathogen's production of the plant hormone, gibberellin..... </task>

<title type="goal" level="2">COMMENTS ON THE DISEASE </title>
Bakanae is one of the oldest known diseases of rice in Asia but has only been observed in California rice since 1999 and now occurs in all California rice-growing regions. While very damaging in Asia, the extent to which Bakanae may effect California rice production is unknown. As diseased plants .....

<title type="goal" level="2">MANAGEMENT</title>
<task type = "PROC">
The most effective means to<action> treat <theme> this disease </theme> </action> is the <instruction compound><instruction type="imperative">use of noninfested seed</instruction>. Also,<connector type="advice"> when possible</connector>, <advice>burning plant residues</advice> with known infection in fall may help limit the disease. ..... Field trials indicate that a seed treatment with sodium hypochlorite (Ultra Clorox Germicidal Bleach) is effective at reducing the incidence of this disease.... </instruction compound> </task>

4.3 Matching selected texts with questions: the deep indexing level

The main words of the question focus and body are used to select a subset of indexed texts as potential candidates containing the response. Then, in each of these texts, the few sentences where the terms of the question or derived terms (closely related terms) are effectively found are annotated by means of semantic roles as for the question, for further analysis and investigations.

For that purpose, we have developed guidelines for annotating those text fragments where the response is and the associated knowledge, based on the same semantic roles as those used in the questions. These annotations remain so far exploratory, in terms of feasibility and automation. Our major concern is to develop a method for annotators so that a large number of texts can be tagged homogeneously and also so that the technique can be reproduced for other technical areas. Finally, in terms of response identification, the goal is to define a metric that defines the best match and selects the text fragment(s) that best respond(s) to the question among several potential candidates.

Let us first consider a simple example. Given the question:

Q8: *"How to eradicate Bakanae ?"*

with the following representation:

<question type="PROC or SqE" focus "eradicate Bakanae" > How to <action> eradicate <theme> Bakanae </theme> </action> ? </question>

The main terms of the question are 'eradicate' and 'Bakanae'. The text above is therefore selected on the basis of its indexes, because 'treatment' is a closely related term (in terms of semantic relation: 'way to realize an event') of 'eradicate' in the domain ontology.

Then, the question terms are searched in the selected text and the sentences that contain them are annotated using semantic roles. For example, the following sentence is a candidate:

The most effective means to treat this disease is the use of noninfested seeds.

It is tagged as:

...<action> treat <theme> this disease </theme> is the use of <instrument> noninfested seeds </instrument> </action> .

The answer is the above sentence and the text fragment that follows (introduced by the connector also) since the response is of type *procedure*:

The most effective means to treat this disease is the use of noninfested seed. Also, when possible, burning plant residues with known infection in fall may help limit the disease.

Following [5], this structure is annotated as a single instructional compound, which is the fundamental unit in a procedural text. This is the structure which is typically returned to users.

Let us present here another illustrative example of a text fragment where the response is annotated together with the required related reasoning elements:

Q9: *"How can thrips destroy the rice ?"*

annotation:

<question type="SqE" focus = "destroy">How can <agent> thrips </agent> <action>destroy <theme>the rice</theme> </action>?</question>

The text fragment that corresponds to the answer is annotated as follows:

<response> <agent> The rice thrips</agent> <action> sucks the sap <source> from the young plant. </source> </action> </response>

To match the action 'destroy' in the question with the text portion from which the response is extracted, it is then necessary to identify the inference:

<lex_inference> <action> Suck sap of X </action> <entail> <modality> probably </modality> <action> destroy X </action> </entail> , <type> X : plant </type> <part-of> sap : X </part-of > </lex inference>

This example shows that (1) in the question and in the answer, annotations are used to identify the different components, arguments, adjuncts, but also some other components (e.g. temporal adverbs), and (2) the annotation is developed to characterize the matching steps and inferential components (either lexical or domain knowledge) between the question and the answer. This latter form of annotation, which is quite time-consuming to develop, is the means we use to induce and develop domain dependent forms of lexical inference (or other phenomena like synonymy, lexical equivalence, etc.) and relevant domain knowledge. The types and lexical functions which are introduced are then used in the process of induction of generalizations over some semantic categories (plants, products, etc.), and verb classes. This way of annotating knowledge and inferences is obviously a simple bottom-up process, with well known limitations, but we feel it may have some advantages for inducing an upper organization of knowledge, in conjunction, and as a complement to, the domain ontology. It is also simple and accessible to annotators. Obviously this remains to be evaluated.

4.4 Generalizing inferences for question-answer matching

At this level, the inferences which may be drawn are directly attached to the terms which are tagged. This is obviously too limited. We are now experimenting with different generalization strategies in order to tune the lexical inference rules. This process involves:

(1) developing various generic principles over different types and categories (via the domain ontology), We will annotation the title for matching the "theme" of the answer to the "theme" and "Focus" of the question by using word net and ontology as shown below.

Surface Form	Concept
destroy, destruct, eliminate, kill,...	destroy
treat, prevent, eradicate, protect,...	manage
suck, eat, bite, drink,...	consume
spread out, diffuse, disperse,...	spread

(2) a set of principles that limit these generalizations via, for example, the taking into account of the semantics restrictions imposed by lexical items, in particular verbs. The main words of the question focus and text body that already annotated will be considered for extracting the potential candidates containing the response. The sentences, where the terms of the question or derived terms (closely related terms) are effectively found, will be the corresponding answer by using matching function as shown below.

```
Function Matching (Question Q, Answer A){
   Match = false;
  // Relevant document
  If (Q.focus  =  A.index)  then
       // Relevant answer
       If  (Q.type =  A.task type) then
           //Detect Answer for the Question
           If (Q.focus = A.title) then
              Match = true;
           Else if (Q.action = A.action and
                  Q.theme = A.theme or
                  Q.agent = A.agent) then
              Match = true;
           End If
       End If
   End If
Return Match;}
```

The tuning of the level of these generalizations is obviously one main parameter of our project. It has several conceptual dimensions that we explore and may also be domain dependent.

Perspectives

The matching problem between questions and documents to retrieve answers in question-answering systems in concrete applicative contexts is often a difficult problem. This matching procedure often requires very accurate domain knowledge, besides ontological descriptions. It is not always easy to access this knowledge in a structured way or to extract it from texts. The present contribution, still experimental and in an early stage of development, is an attempt, via annotations, at resolving this problem, following a simple and clear methodology.

This task needs to be developed and evaluated gradually. So far, it is too early to evaluate the quality of the generalizations and the inferential patterns we get.

This approach, and the principles we have briefly outlined, allow us to introduce a working method for the development of question-answering systems for concrete applications, especially for non-factoid questions, an area which is still not very much developed in spite of its obvious usefulness. One of the reasons is that non-factoid questions require a language processing technology, analysis methods, reasoning aspects, and a conceptual approach, which are substantially different from what is used for factoid questions.

Acknowledgments

The work described in this paper has been supported by the NECTEC No. NT-B-22-KE-12-50-19, within the project, "I-KnowII: CAT, EAT, RATs," and "Agricultural Question & Answering Service System," granted by the KURDI, Kasetsart University. We would like to especially thank Prof. Patrick Saint Dizier for originating, advising and collaborating in the development of Q&A system. We also thank Prof. William I. Grosky for helping to revise our English.

References

1. Asanee Kawtrakul, et al. Chaveevan Pechsiri, Sachit Rajbhandari, Frederic Andres, Problems-Solving Map Extraction with Collective Intelligence Analy-sis and Language Engineering , Book Chapter 18, Medical Information Science Reference in Information Retrieval in Biomedicine ISBN: 978-1-60566-274-9; pp 460

2. Asanee Kawtrakul, et al. 2009. From CyberBrain to Q&A Services: A Development of Question - Answering Services System for the Farmer through the SMS, WCCA2009, Grand Sierra Resort, Reno, Nevada, USA.

3. Asanee Kawtrakul, et al. 2008. "CyberBrain: Towards the Next Generation Social Intelligence" IAALD AFITA WCCA 2008, Tokyo, Japan.

4. Dan Moldovan, Sanda Harabagiu, Marius Pasca, Rada Mihalcea, Roxana Girju, Richard Goodrum, Vasile Rus. 2000. The Structure and Performance of an Open-Domain Question Answering System, Proceedings of the 38th Meeting of the Association for Computational Linguistics (ACL), Hong Kong.

5. Estelle Delpech, Patrick Saint-Dizier. 2008. Investigating the Structure of Procedural Texts for Answering How-to Questions, LREC2008, Marrakech.

6. Jochen L. Leidner, 2005. A wireless natural language search engine. Proceedings of the 28th annual international ACM SIGIR conference on Research and development in information retrieval table of contents: 677 – 677, ACM, New York, USA

7. Judy Delin, Anthony Hartley, Cecile Paris, Donia Scott, Keith Vander Linden. 1994. Expressing Procedural Relation-ships in Multilingual Instructions, Proceedings of the 7th International Workshop on Natural Language Generation: 61-70, Maine, USA.

8. Karen Sparck Jones, Branimir Boguraev.1987. A note on a study of cases, research note in Computational Linguistics archive, Volume 13 , Issue 1-2 (January-June 1987) : 65 - 68.

9. Leonard Talmy. 1976. Semantic Causative Types, In M. Shibatani (ed.), Syntax and Semantics 6: The Grammar of Causative Constructions. New York: Academic Press: 43-116.

10. Leonard Talmy. 1985. Lexicalization Patterns: Seman-tic Structure in Lexical Forms, in Language Typol-ogy and Syntactic Description 3: Grammatical Categories and the Lexicon, T. Shopen(ed.), 57-149, Cambridge University Press.

11. Mark Thomas Maybury. 2004. New Directions in Question Answering, The MIT Press, Menlo Park.

12. Mineki Takechi, Takenobu Tokunaga, Yuji Matsumoto, Hozumi Tanaka. 2003. Feature Selection in Categorizing Procedural Expressions, The 6th International Workshop on Information Retrieval with Asian Languages (IRAL2003):49-56.

13. Ray Jackendoff. 1990. Semantic Structures, MIT Press.

14. Robert E. Longacre. 1982. Discourse Typology in Relation to Language Typology, Sture Allen ́ed., Text Processing, Proceeding of Nobel Symposium 51, Stockholm, Almquist and Wiksell, 457-486.

15. Sadhu Balasundaram Ramakishnan and Balakrishnan Ramadoss. 2007. SMS for Question-Answering in the m-Learning Scena-rio, Journal of Computer Science 3(2):119-121.

QAST: Question Answering System for Thai Wikipedia

Wittawat Jitkrittum† **Choochart Haruechaiyasak**‡ **Thanaruk Theeramunkong**†

†School of Information, Computer and Communication Technology (ICT)
Sirindhorn International Institute of Technology (SIIT)
131 Moo 5 Tiwanont Rd., Bangkadi, Muang, Phathumthani, Thailand, 12000
wittawatj@gmail.com, thanaruk@siit.tu.ac.th

‡Human Language Technology Laboratory (HLT)
National Electronics and Computer Technology Center (NECTEC)
Thailand Science Park, Klong Luang, Pathumthani 12120, Thailand
choochart.haruechaiyasak@nectec.or.th

Abstract

We propose an open-domain question answering system using Thai Wikipedia as the knowledge base. Two types of information are used for answering a question: (1) structured information extracted and stored in the form of Resource Description Framework (RDF), and (2) unstructured texts stored as a search index. For the structured information, SPARQL transformed query is applied to retrieve a short answer from the RDF base. For the unstructured information, keyword-based query is used to retrieve the shortest text span containing the questions's key terms. From the experimental results, the system which integrates both approaches could achieve an average MRR of 0.47 based on 215 test questions.

1 Introduction

Most keyword-based search engines available online do not support the retrieval of precise information. They only return a list of URLs, each referring to a web page, sorted by relevancy to the user's query. Users then have to manually scan those documents for needed information. Due to this limitation, many techniques for implementing QA systems have been proposed in the past decades.

From the literature reviews, previous and existing QA systems can be broadly categorized into two types:

1. **Knowledge Intensive:** Knowledge intensive systems focus on analyzing and understanding the input questions. The system knows exactly what to be answered, and also what type the answer should be. The analysis phase usually depends on an ontology or a semantic lexicon like WordNet. The answer is retrieved from a predefined organized knowledge base. Natural Language Processing (NLP) techniques are heavily used in a knowledge intensive system.
2. **Data Intensive:** Data intensive systems, which do not fully analyze the input questions, rely on the redundancy of huge amount of data (Dumais et al., 2002). The idea is that if we have a huge amount of data, a piece of information is likely to be stated more than once in different forms. As a result, the data-intensive QA systems are not required to perform many complex NLP techniques.

In this paper, we propose an open-domain QA system for Thai Wikipedia called QAST. The system supports five types of close-ended questions: *person*, *organization*, *place*, *quantity*, and *date/-time*. Our system can be classified as a data intensive type with an additional support of structured information. Structured information in Thai Wikipedia is extracted and represented in the form of RDF. We use SPARQL to retrieve specific information from the RDF base. If using SPARQL cannot answer a given question, the system will retrieve answer candidates from the pre-constructed search index using a technique based on Minimal Span Weighting (Monz, 2003).

2 System Architecture

Figure 1 shows the system architecture of QAST which consists of three main sub-systems: *Data Representation*, *Question Processor*, and *Answer*

Proceedings of the 2009 Workshop on Knowledge and Reasoning for Answering Questions, ACL-IJCNLP 2009, pages 11–14, Suntec, Singapore, 6 August 2009.

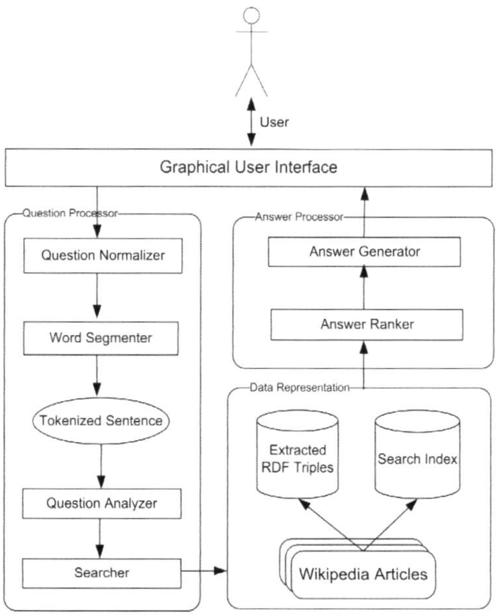

Figure 1: The system architecture of QAST

Processor.

2.1 Data Representation

The *Data Representation* part is a storage for all information contained in Thai Wikipedia. Two modules constitute this sub-system.

RDF Base: In QAST, RDF triples are generated from Wikipedia's infoboxes following similar approaches described in the works of Isbell and Butler (2007) and Auer and Lehmann (2007). To generate RDF triples from an infobox, we would have the article title as the subject. The predicates are the keys in the first column. The objects are the values in the second column. Altogether, the number of generated triples corresponds to the number of rows in the infobox.

In addition to the infoboxes, we also store synonyms in the form of RDF triples. The synonyms are extracted from redirect pages in Wikipedia. For example, a request for the Wikipedia article titled "Car" will result in another article titled "Automobile" to be shown up. The former page usually has no content and only acts as a pointer to another page which contains the full content. The relationship of these two pages implies that "Car" and "Automobile" are synonymous. Synonyms are useful in retrieving the same piece of information with different texual expressions.

Search Index: QAST stores the textual content as a search index. We used the well-known IR library, Lucene[1], for our search backend. We indexed 41,512 articles (as of February 5, 2009) from a Thai Wikipedia dump with full term positions. Firstly, all template constructs and the WikiText markups are removed, leaving with only the plain texts. A dictionary-based longest-matching word segmentation is then performed to tokenize the plain texts into series of terms. Finally, the resulted list of non-stopwords are passed to the Lucene indexing engine. The dictionary used for word segmentation is a combination of word list from the LEX*i*TRON[2] and all article titles from Thai Wikipedia. In total, there are 81,345 words in the dictionary.

2.2 Question Processor

Question processor sub-system consists of four modules as follows.

1. **Question Normalizer** – This first module is to change the way the question is formed into a normal form to ease the processing at latter stages. This includes correcting mistyped words or unusual spelling such as *f33t* for *feet*.
2. **Word Segmenter** – This module performs tokenizing on the normalized question to obtain a list of non-stopwords.
3. **Question Analyzer** – The question analyzer determines the expected type of answer (i.e., quantity, person, organization, location, date/time and unknown) and constructs an appropriate query. Normally, a SPARQL query is generated and used to retrieve a candidate answer from the RDF base. When the SPARQL fails to find an answer, the system will switch to the index search. In that case, the module also defines a set of hint terms to help in locating candidate answers.
4. **Searcher** – This module executes the query and retrieves candidate answers from the data representation part.

To generate a SPARQL query, the input question is compared against a set of predefined regular expression patterns. Currently, the system has two types of patterns: pattern for definitional questions, and pattern for questions asking for a prop-

[1]Apache Lucene, `http://lucene.apache.org`
[2]LEX*i*TRON, `http://lexitron.nectec.or.th`

erty of an entity. The pattern for definitional question is of the form a-rai-kue-X 'What is X ?' or X-kue-a-rai 'X is what ?'. After X is determined from a user's question, the first paragraph of the article titled X is retrieved and directly returned to the user. Since the first paragraph in any article is usually the summary, it is appropriate to use the first paragraph to answer a definitional question.

Questions asking for a property of an entity are of the form a-rai-kue-P-kong-X 'What is P of X ?' e.g., "When was SIIT established ?" which can be answered by looking for the right information in the RDF base. A simplified SPARQL query used to retrieve an answer for this type of question is as follows.

```
SELECT ?o
WHERE {
  ?tempPage hasInfobox ?tempBox .
  ?tempPage rdfs:label "X" .
  ?tempBox ?P ?o .
}
```

The query matches an object of a RDF triple with the predicate P (e.g., "date of establishment"), provided that the triple is generated from an infobox titled X (e.g.,"SIIT") . The object of the year 1992 is then correctly returned as the answer.

When SPARQL fails, i.e., the question does not match any known pattern or the answer does not exist in the RDF base, the system switches to the index search which performs the following the steps.

1. Word Segmenter tokenizes the question into a list of keywords q.
2. Question analyzer analyzes q, generates a basic Lucene' *TermQuery*, and defines a set of hint terms H.
3. Retrieve the most relevant c documents using Lucene's default search scoring function[3]. Denote D as the set of retrieved documents.
4. For each document d in D where $d = \{t_1, t_2, \ldots, t_{|d|}\}$ (t is a term),
   (a) Find in d the start term index $mmsStart$ and end term index $mmsEnd$ of the shortest term span containing all terms in q (Monz, 2003).
   (b) $spanLength \leftarrow 1 + mmsEnd - mmsStart$
   (c) If $spanLength > 30$, skip current d. Go to the next document.
   (d) Find minimal span weighting score msw (Monz, 2003). If $|q \cap d| = 1$ then, $msw = RSV_n(q,d)$. Otherwise, $msw = 0.4 \cdot RSV_n(q,d) + 0.6 \cdot (\frac{|q \cap d|}{spanLength})^{1/8} \cdot (\frac{|q \cap d|}{|q|})$ where $RSV_n(q,d) = lucene(q,d)/max_d lucene(q,d)$
   (e) $mmsStart \leftarrow max(mmsStart - s, 1)$
   (f) $mmsEnd \leftarrow min(mmsEnd + s, |d|)$
   (g) Find the weighting for hint terms hw $(0 \leq hw \leq 1)$.
   (h) Calculate the span score $sp = msw \cdot (1 + hw)$
   (i) Add the text span to the span set P (Sort P by sp in descending order).
5. Return the top k spans in P as answers.

In the actual implementation, we set c equal to 500 so that only the top 500 documents are considered. Although retrieving more texts from the corpus would likely increase the chance of finding the answer (Moldovan et al., 2002), our trial-and-error showed that 500 documents seem to be a good trade-off between speed and content coverage. To look for an occurrence of hint terms, each span is stretched backward and forward for 10 terms (i.e., $s = 10$). Finally, we set k equal to 5 to return only the top five spans as the answers.

2.3 Answer Processor

This sub-system contains two modules: *Answer Ranker* and *Answer Generator*.

Answer Ranker concerns with how to rank the retrieved answer candidates. In the case where SPARQL query is used, this module is not required since most of the time there will be only one result returned.

In the case when the search index is used, all candidate answers are sorted by the heuristic span score (i.e., $sp = msw \cdot (1 + hw)$). The function mostly relies on regular expressions defining expected answer patterns. If a span has an occurrence of one of the defined patterns (i.e., $hw > 0$), it is directly proportional to the suitability of the occurrence with respect to the question, length and rareness of the pattern occurrence. For example, the hint terms of questions asking for a person would be personal titles such as Ms. and Dr.

As for the final step, the Answer Generator module formats the top five candidate answers into an HTML table and returns the results to the user.

[3]http://lucene.apache.org/java/2_3_0/scoring.html

Question Type	Index & RDF	Index
Person	0.47	0.37
Organization	0.56	0.46
Place/Location	0.43	0.36
Quantity	0.51	0.44
Date/Time	0.39	0.34
Average MRR	**0.47**	0.39

Table 1: QAST's performance comparison between (1) using both index and RDF and (2) using only the index.

3 Evaluation Metric

To evaluate the system, 215 test questions (43 questions for each question type) and their correct answers were constructed based on the contents of random articles in Thai Wikipedia. Mean Reciprocal Rank (MRR), the official measurement used for QA systems in TREC (Voorhees and Tice, 2000), is used as the performance measurement. To evaluate the system, a question is said to be correctly answered only when at least one of the produced five ranked candidates contained the true answer with the right context. Out-of-context candidate phrases which happen to contain the true answers are not counted. If there is no correct answer in any candidate, the score for that question is equal to zero.

4 Experimental Results and Discussion

Table 1 shows a comparison of the MRR values when using both index and RDF, and using only the index. The approach of using only the index, the overall MRR is equal to 0.39 which is fairly high with respect to the answer retrieval methodology. The index search approach simply relies on the fact that if the question keywords in a ranked candidate document occur close together and at least one occurrence of expected answer pattern exists, then there is a high chance that the term span contains an answer.

The MRR significantly increases to 0.47 (20.5% improvement) when RDF (structured information) is used together with the index. A thorough analysis showed that out of 215 questions, 21 questions triggered the RDF base. Among these, 18 questions were correctly answered. Therefore, using the additional structured information helps answer the definitional and factoid questions. We expect a higher improvement when more structured information is incorporated into the system.

5 Conclusions and Future Works

We proposed an open-domain QA system called QAST. The system uses Thai Wikipedia as the corpus and does not rely on any complex NLP technique in retrieving an answer.

As for future works, some possiblities for improving the current QAST are as follows.

- An information extraction module may be added to extract and generate RDF triples from unstructured text.
- Infoboxes, wikipedia categories and internal article links may be further explored to construct an ontology which will allow an automatic type inference of entities.
- More question patterns and the corresponding SPARQL queries can be added so that SPARQL is used more often.

Acknowledgement

The financial support from Young Scientist and Technologist Programme, NSTDA (YSTP : SP-51-NT-15) is gratefully acknowledged.

References

Soren Auer and Jens Lehmann. 2007. *What Have Innsbruck and Leipzig in Common? Extracting Semantics from Wiki Content*. In Proc. of the 4th European conference on The Semantic Web: Research and Applications, pp. 503-517.

Susan Dumais, Michele Banko, Eric Brill, Jimmy Lin, and Andrew Ng. 2002. *Web Question Answering: Is More Always Better?*. In Proc. of the 25th ACM SIGIR, pp. 291-298.

Jonathan Isbell and Mark H. Butler. 2007. *Extracting and Re-using Structured Data from Wikis*. Technical Report HPL-2007-182, Hewlett-Packard.

Dan Moldovan, Marius Pasca, Sanda Harabagiu, and Mihai Surdeanu . 2002. *Performance Issues and Error Analysis in an Open-Domain Question Answering System*. Proc. of the 40th ACL, pp. 33-40.

Christof Monz. 2003. *From Document Retrieval to Question Answering*. Ph.D. Thesis. University of Amsterdam.

Ellen M. Voorhees and Dawn Tice. 2000. *Building a Question Answering Test Collection*. In 23rd ACM SIGIR, pp. 200-207.

Some Challenges in the Design of Comparative and Evaluative Question Answering Systems

Nathalie Rose Lim
De La Salle University-Manila
2401 Taft Avenue, Philippines
Université Paul Sabatier
118 route de Narbonne, France
nats.lim@delasalle.ph

Patrick Saint-Dizier
IRIT-Université Paul Sabatier
118 route de Narbonne,
Toulouse, France
stdizier@irit.fr

Rachel Roxas
De La Salle University-Manila
2401 Taft Avenue,
Manila, Philippines
rachel.roxas@dlsu.edu.ph

Abstract

Comparative and evaluative question answering (QA) requires a detailed semantic analysis of comparative expressions and complex processing. Semantics of predicates from questions have to be translated to quantifiable criteria before extraction of information can be done. This paper presents some challenges faced in answering comparative and evaluative questions. An application on the domain of business intelligence is discussed.

1 Introduction

In the recently updated paper by Burger, et al. (2009), it is indicated that new types of questions like evaluative and comparative questions must be targeted in question answering (QA) systems. Evaluative refers to the consideration of at least one property or criteria over one or more entities and the computation of the associated values. Comparative refers to the evaluation of objects depending on one or more criteria and classifying those objects depending on the returned values. Included in comparative is the identification of the extreme, i.e., the superlatives, the topmost objects. In such cases, the focus of the questions is on the properties at stake in the evaluation, leading to the comparison. Thus, comparative and evaluative QA involves answering questions that require various forms of inference related to evaluation before an answer can be given. Since evaluation is necessary, the answer is not lifted from source text, as in the case of answering factoid, definition, or list questions. Instead, natural language answers will have to be constructed from the results of numeric and non-numeric evaluations of the criteria.

Currently, to our knowledge, there are no systems that answer comparative and evaluative questions. The closest applications to comparing or evaluating information are implemented through natural language database interfaces (Olawsky, 1989) and database queries (e.g., via SQL statements). In the former, the user is prompted to choose among a set of candidate interpretations of comparative expressions to indicate his intent. The comparisons are based on quantifiable predicates (i.e., those measurable by count, mass, or value). Using database queries restrict the possible questions that can be raised and is far less natural and user-friendly than using human language. It also does not allow producing cooperative responses.

Recent researches in linguistics on the semantics of comparatives and superlatives (Kennedy, 2006) can be used as a basis in answering comparative and evaluative questions. The next section discusses some challenges we have identified as crucial for the development of comparative and evaluative QA systems. We briefly propose some research directions we have explored or evaluated. We end this short document by a few illustrations from two applications we have worked on during the past year.

2 Challenges

The processes involved in classic components of a QA system are not only more complex but different for comparative and evaluative QA.

2.1 Question Analysis and Semantics of Comparatives

A question analyzer must identify the comparative expressions in the question and decompose it into meaningful constituents, among which are those properties that will be evaluated and the parameters of the comparison. Issues include:

- Identifying the type of comparison
Comparisons may be in relation to properties within the same object, degree of comparisons of the same property between different objects, or

Proceedings of the 2009 Workshop on Knowledge and Reasoning for Answering Questions, ACL-IJCNLP 2009, pages 15–18, Suntec, Singapore, 6 August 2009. ©2009 ACL and AFNLP

different properties of different objects (Kennedy, 2006). In some simple situations, comparative relations in sentences can be extracted automatically via machine learning (Jindal and Liu, 2006). Their approach determines whether the expression is non-equal gradable, equative, or superlative. From this, the type of comparison may be determined from the semantics of the predicate and the properties of the objects through the pairability constraints. In our approach, we want to explore in more depth semantic and conceptual issues and their dependence to context, users, and domains.

- Determining semantic meaning and converting to quantifiable measures
The properties at stake in the comparison are embedded in the semantics of the words in the question, and possibly in the context that comes with the question. To date, there is obviously no widely available lexical resource containing an exhaustive list of comparative predicates, applied to precise terms, together with the properties involved. These can possibly be derived, to a limited extent, from existing resources like FrameNet or from an ontology where relationships between concepts and terms can be mapped. However, this is tractable for very simple situations, and in most cases, identifying those properties is a major challenge. We plan to explore, over restricted domains, ways to accurately identify those properties through different resources (like Generative Lexicon) and elaborate on inferential models to associate properties for evaluation.

- Determining limits, ranges, and values that are relative depending on the object
The standard of comparison (i.e., the value) associated to the predicate may be different based on the context, i.e., depending on the object that it is associated to and on the type of predicate. Properties of predicates may be underspecified and/or polysemic and would gain context only when associated with the object. One such predicate is *innovative*. The following are some properties that can be used to evaluate *innovative*.

- innovative product: type of product, number of entities interested in acquiring the product
- innovative company: strategy employed, type of product it produces
- innovative research: number of papers published on the same research, number of citations from other authors

To automatically determine the properties, including default values, to be used in the evaluation, other available sources indicating some range of values may be tapped, as is done in answer fusion (Girju, 2001). But rather than retrieving the partial answer, properties needed for evaluation must be retrieved or inferred. In terms of values, we have either numerical values (where comparisons are quite easy to handle) or textual values (that are often discrete). It is then necessary to define comparative scales along basic properties so that those values get ordered. This is a major challenge for our project.

- Processing superlatives and other forms of quantification related to comparisons
Superlatives and other forms of quantifications in connection with comparative expressions can also be used on top of the basic evaluative expressions. As the semantics of the predicate may encompass multiple properties, strict evaluation of these may trim the list prematurely. Consider the question:

- Which companies *take* the *most risk*?

Take most risk entails different dimensions from being *conservative*. In the context of business intelligence, evaluation could be in terms of the amount of investments, types of products invested in, the partners being taken, or all of these criteria. If a strict evaluation of all these criteria is done, the result may not be complete or accurate. We are exploring on relaxing the evaluation of multiple properties before determining the top results and on evaluating the superlative of each of the properties so as to identify which of the properties the object has not met.

2.2 Answer Determination

Only when the predicate/s is/are decomposed into properties can proper evaluation take place. We have two situations: either the QA system is connected to a database (which may have been constructed from natural language data as in the case of economic news) or it searches for the response on the Web. In the first case, the main challenge is to convert the concepts of the query into those of the conceptual schema of the database.

In the second case, relevant data must be searched on the Web. A straightforward procedure consists of extracting keywords from the question, then getting results from search engines from which, via local grammars associated to properties, relevant values may be extracted. We already successfully conducted such an experiment for numerical data fusion (Moriceau, 2006).

2.3 Response Generation

The answer cannot be lifted from the source text, thus a response generator component should be part of a comparative and evaluative QA system. As response is to be generated from the results of numeric and textual comparisons of the criteria, it is necessary to go through complex sentence generation, involving comparative expressions. In case the response is not direct, it is also necessary to elaborate adapted forms of cooperativity, by providing the user with adequate forms of explanations, elaborations, examples (of properties), and other relevant information. This is clearly a major challenge, since the quality of the response will reflect the overall credibility of the system.

3 Applications

We first carried out a relatively simple experiment on the business intelligence domain, where the criteria for evaluation are almost an exact science. The difficulty is to get the expertise in economics and to formulate it in terms of properties "visible" in the related economic news. An example question is given in (1).

1. `Which private biotech companies in Asia have the highest number of transactions from 2005 to 2008?`

News articles are used as the source of information to answer these types of questions. They are factual, structured, and concise. They do not contain conflicting information, though there is the possibility of updates but the date is normally included in the information to provide temporal perspective. Rhetorical relations between sentences are being explored to give hints as to the relevance of information in the sentences. Semantic dependencies via thematic roles of arguments within each sentence are being considered to extract data. From the semantic dependency representation, a conceptual representation of these information is created using type-feature structure with the following information:

```
[ News        [ Source
                Location
                Date
                Link ]
  Transaction [ TransCategory
                TransType
                Date
                Location
                Company (1..10)
                ContractedItem ] ]
```

Location and Date are complex types containing info like country and month, respectively. TransCategory and TransType are transaction categories and its transaction subtype. There can be at most ten companies, where each contains information like the name and location of the company. The ContractedItem is also a complex type containing information like worth of the product.

To build this knowledge base, other web sources are used and a set of inferencing rules is developed to retrieve and store the required information.

Similarly, questions are represented semantically using thematic roles. Then, a conceptual representation is built to map the question focus with the answer from the type-feature representation of the news. To illustrate, the question type-feature structure contains the following:

```
Question [ Question Type          Search Contraints
           Number of Results      [ Duration [ DateStart
           Search Criteria                     DateEnd ]
           Question Focus           Location
           Search Constraints ]     Transaction ]
```

For criteria or properties that are already in the conceptual representation, these are used in the evaluation and/or comparison. For question (1), occurrences of each company that fit the constraints (e.g., location Asia), are counted and the resulting values are compared to determine the top companies.

However, in (2), the sample question involves a non-directly translatable predicate.

2. `Does Company X take more risks than Company Y?`

Non-directly translatable predicates can be quantifiable by one criterion (e.g., active company: company with above-mean number of transactions), quantifiable by multiple criteria (e.g., company that take-risk: active company that has transactions every year, and has alliances every year but always with new partners or has unstable partners), polysemous (e.g., stable can mean ability to resist motion, steady in purpose, or established), and/or underspecified (e.g., stable company vs. stable partner, though partner is also a company, the criteria is not the same. Stable company is an active company that may not have alliances every year or have alliances every year but always with old partners, whereas a stable partner is a company with alliances every year). There is also the issue of metonymy. In the context of company, the set of quantifiable properties associated to company could be number of employees, number of transactions, type of partners, and so on. Choosing which of these properties to associate to evaluate a predicate (like *stable*) is a challenge.

In this application, the categories, classifications, boundaries (what the term entails), and evaluation criteria of the terms are defined by an expert, so the result is consistent and objective. The challenge is to analyze the given information and convert it to machine tractable instructions. At present, set theory is used to define constraints and to generate the answer. It should be noted that it is one expert's interpretation of the terminologies used in the constraints. Others may have different criteria to associate with the predicates.

Other domains, like tourism, may be more challenging. Aside from information sources being not purely textual (i.e., some may be in tables or diagrams), the evaluation criteria for questions (3) and (4) may be subjective and may produce conflicting results. For example, value for money is subjective since certain amenities may not be important to the user. This can be resolved by prompting the user for additional criteria, by having a user profile, or by comparing with other entities (in this case, other hotels) to determine what is considered the norm (as a gauge to what is exceptional). It is also possible to generate different results based on the various criteria and present these to the user with explanations on the basis used.

3. `Which hotels in Singapore offer the most value for money for stay from August 28, 2009?`

4. `Which Asian cities are most kid-friendly?`

5. `Which hotels in Asia are most kid-friendly?`

As mentioned, the properties at stake in the evaluation could be different if the question focus was changed, as in the case of "kid-friendly" in question (5). In question (4), the criteria for a kid-friendly city could be one with avenues for fun and entertainment (like theme parks, zoos, parks) and a city with low crime rate (or specifically, low child abuse rate). On the other hand, a kid-friendly hotel would be one with amenities for supervised or planned activities, proximity to entertainment venues, larger rooms, or special menu for kids. The criteria or properties cannot be easily and reliably accessed from an ontology. Our challenge here is to elaborate means to get those properties. A direction we are investigating includes learning these properties from the web, but we may be faced with the recurrent problem of data sparseness, besides the fact that the web contains many erroneous statements.

Acknowledgments

The authors would like to thank Prof. Brigitte Gay of Ecole Superieure de Commerce - Toulouse for her invaluable inputs regarding comparative and evaluative questions in business intelligence.

References

John Burger, et al. 2009. *Issues, Tasks and Program Structures to Roadmap Research in Question & Answering.* Available in: www-nlpir.nist.gov/projects/duc/papers/qa.Roadmap-paper_v2.doc.

Roxana Girju. 2001. *Answer Fusion with On-line Ontology Development.* In Students Research Workshop of the Second Meeting of the North American Chapter of the ACL. Available in: lyle.smu.edu/~roxana/papers/NAACL01.ps.

Nitin Jindal and Bing Liu. 2006. *Mining Comparative Sentences and Relations.* In Proceedings of the 21st AAAI Conference on Artificial Intelligence. AAAI Press, California,USA.

Christopher Kennedy. 2006. *Comparatives, Semantics Of.* In K. Allen (section editor) Lexical and Logical Semantics; Encyclopedia of Language and Linguistics, 2nd Edition. Elsevier, Oxford.

Véronique Moriceau. 2006. *Numeric Data Integration for Cooperative Question-Answering.* In Proceedings of the Knowledge and Reasoning for Language Processing Workshop (KRAQ 2006). ACL, Italy.

Duane Olawsky. 1989. *The Lexical Semantics of Comparative Expressions in a Multi-level Semantic Processor.* In Proceedings of the 27th Annual Meeting on ACL. ACL, USA.

Addressing How-to Questions using a Spoken Dialogue System: a Viable Approach?

Silvia Quarteroni
University of Trento
38050 Povo (Trento), Italy
silviaq@disi.unitn.it

Patrick Saint-Dizier
IRIT
Toulouse, France
stdizier@irit.fr

Abstract

In this document, we illustrate how complex questions such as procedural (how-to) ones can be addressed in an interactive format by means of a spoken dialogue system. The advantages of interactivity and in particular of spoken dialogue with respect to standard Question Answering settings are numerous. First, addressing user needs that do not necessarily arise in front of a computer; moreover, a spoken or multimodal answer format can often be better suited to the user's need. Finally, the procedural nature of the information itself makes iterative question formulation and answer production particularly appealing.

1 Introduction

Question answering (QA) is nowadays an established technology, advancing information retrieval to the point of allowing queries to be formulated in natural language and to return actual answers (in the form of sentences/phrases).

While the first QA systems (Simmons, 1965) mainly dealt with factoid questions, i.e. questions about names, dates and all that can be reduced to a fact, a number of systems in the last decade have appeared with the aim of addressing non-factoid questions (Voorhees, 2003). In particular, the problem of addressing definition questions has received great attention from the research community (Chen et al., 2006; Moschitti et al., 2007), while less research has been conducted so far on other types of non-factoid QA, such as *why*-questions (Verberne et al., 2007; Pechsiri et al., 2008) and procedural (also called *how-to*) questions (Yin, 2006; Delpech and Saint-Dizier, 2008).

Another recent trend in QA is interactivity, i.e. the use of a dialogue interface to better support the user, e.g. by resolving anaphoric and elliptic expressions in his/her queries (Webb and Strzalkowski, 2006). Indeed, the dialogue community has been addressing the problem of information seeking for decades, often with very satisfying commercial products able to interact not only in text but especially via spoken interfaces (Gupta et al., 2006; Traum, 1996). However, also in this field the information retrieval task has mainly focused on a limited domain (travel planning, telecom rates) and on returning database values rather than cooperatively solving problems or providing complex information.

In this paper, we focus on handling procedural questions, not as commonly researched as definitional QA but for which a number of resources are available on the Web. Indeed, although portals dedicated to how-to questions exist (eHow.com), where stereotyped questions are presented together with a few responses, QA would allow a broader approach to intelligently respond to how-to questions.

Our main claim is that joining the existing QA technology for complex procedural questions with the potentials of spoken conversation would provide an excellent testbed for the integration of these two technologies. Indeed, understanding and answering procedural questions requires a high level of cooperation between the user and the system: a procedure is a complex answer to return and would better be provided and received step by step than "dumped" in a text-to-speech generator or a text file.

In the rest of this document, we outline the main features of procedural QA and the approach we propose to address it via dialogue. We illustrate the potentials of our approach with two use cases of different complexity.

2 Procedural Question Answering

Procedural text contains not only step-by-step instructions, but also additional content such as

Proceedings of the 2009 Workshop on Knowledge and Reasoning for Answering Questions, ACL-IJCNLP 2009, pages 19–23,
Suntec, Singapore, 6 August 2009.

warnings, recommendations and advice. Due to the argumentative nature of such text, procedural QA is a complex task. Indeed, the main challeges offered by procedural QA can be summarized as:

1. Acquiring procedural data:
   - (automatically) obtaining the data, filtering out text with little procedural content;
   - tagging relevant structures in procedures (such as warnings, advice, step-wise instructions);
   - efficiently indexing texts based on their title and content;

2. Answering procedural questions:
   - recognizing and interpreting procedural questions (question classification and analysis);
   - pinpointing answer passages (answer retrieval);
   - generating answers to procedural questions and supporting interaction spanning over more than one Q/A pair, such as step-by-step procedural descriptions.

To our knowledge, little extensive work exists in this field; an example is the TextCoop project (Delpech and Saint-Dizier, 2008) that produced a procedural tagger able to recognize and segment the main units found in French procedural text (titles, instructions, prerequisites, warnings and advice) via an *ad hoc* markup convention (see Table 1). In addition, QA technology was used for the resolution of elliptic titles and their indexing for answer matching (titles often express goals).

Although automatic procedure tagging and analysis appears as a necessary step towards an efficient treatment of procedural questions, we argue that an accurate choice of the format and modality in which their answers are returned would be a vital advantage. In particular, we propose to return the response to a procedural QA under the form of oral instructions rather than text to read. Indeed, besides the advantages of oral communication in terms of expressiveness, the latter solution may be inappropriate in some situations such as when walking around or driving.

In Section 3, we discuss our dialogue-based approach to procedural QA.

3 Dialogue-based Procedural QA

We believe that the integration of QA research with a Spoken Dialogue System (SDS) is a promising approach to procedural Question Answering. Indeed, work on procedural QA so far accounts for the textual structures of written documents; since procedural texts are in general highly interactive, it is clear that the pairing with a spoken dialogue system is of much interest. In addition, a spoken interface enables to go far beyond a mere enumeration of instructions (as found in Web pages), achieving cooperation between the service provider (SDS) and the user.

A first step towards this is the (automatic or semi-automatic) annotation of procedural texts via an *ad hoc* markup in order to distinguish subtexts that can yield to dialogues, such as conditions (texts containing "if you are under 20 . . . ", "if you are aged between . . . " may be translated in the question: "how old are you?"). Similarly, in warnings, terms bearing the illocutionary force ("Remember", "Caution", "Notice") can be marked in order to be stressed.

During system execution, instructions can be uttered one after the other, waiting for an acknowledgement from the user, but the system can also provide more information about the task at hand upon request. Moreover, the system can provide alternative solutions when users have trouble carrying out an instruction ("I cannot pay by credit card"), or make an instruction more explicit by splitting it into simpler ones (automatically generating another how-to question for the subgoal at hand).

Finally, in addition to speech and dialogue, multimodal aspects of interactivity can be considered, such as displaying a map when providing an itinerary, or a 3D picture related to an instruction.

Translating a procedural text into speech is a challenge that requires intensive NLP processing, a strong and accurate domain model and an ability for reasoning. In order to address this challenge, we propose the following approach:

1. Obtain domain-related data from the Web;

2. Represent domain knowledge and reasoning. While most of the factual knowledge of a domain can be captured by means of an enriched ontology, other types of knowledge (know-how, domain constraints, etc.) and

reasoning procedures need to be defined on other grounds, optionally manually;

3. Devise a Dialogue Manager able to interact about procedural information using markup in the procedural data representation;

4. Define how the procedural data representation can be rendered by a Natural Language Generator;

5. Use existing technology for Automatic Speech Recognition and Text-To-Speech.

Evidently, the difficulty of answering procedural questions via dialogue varies depending on the availability and format of answers. We distinguish between two types of questions:

Type 1: a procedural text corresponding to the question is already available on the Web; in this case, the user's query can be answered by tagging such text using a tagger such as TextCoop and enriching it with dialogic and prosodic markers to be rendered by an off-the-shelf TTS module;

Type 2: there is no direct answer to the user's query on the Web; for instance, the answer may be dependent on information which the user has not yet provided. In this case, the query must first be formulated, and procedural tagging/TTS intervene later.

In Sections 4 and 5, we report two case studies reflecting type 1 and type 2 situations, respectively: the first relates to the University helpdesk domain, the second to the tourist advice domain.

4 Text-to-Speech from a Web page

To illustrate type 1 questions, we study a well-known domain, universities, where helpdesks must provide various kinds of procedural information (dealing with e.g. paperwork, student life and infrastructure).Let us consider the question: *"How to get a student card in Wolverhampton?"*. In Fig. 1, we report an extract of the top Web page obtained by typing such question into a search engine. It can be noted that in this case, the top search engine result contains the procedural answer sought by the question, hence procedural tagging can be performed on the text.

A possible procedural annotation has been (manually) applied to the same text in Figure 2,

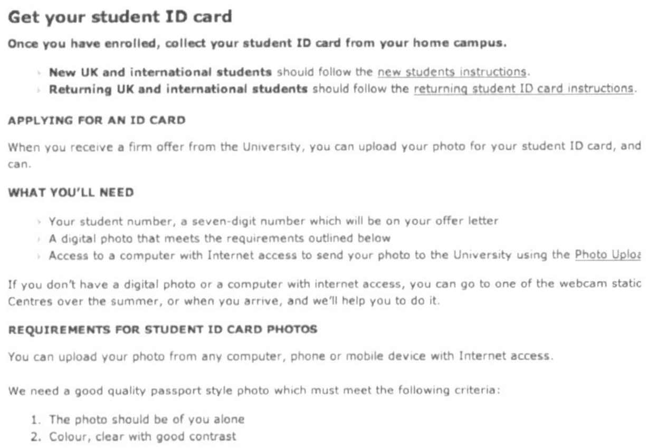
Get your student ID card

Once you have enrolled, collect your student ID card from your home campus.

- **New UK and international students** should follow the new students instructions.
- **Returning UK and international students** should follow the returning student ID card instructions.

APPLYING FOR AN ID CARD

When you receive a firm offer from the University, you can upload your photo for your student ID card, and can.

WHAT YOU'LL NEED

- Your student number, a seven-digit number which will be on your offer letter
- A digital photo that meets the requirements outlined below
- Access to a computer with Internet access to send your photo to the University using the Photo Uploa

If you don't have a digital photo or a computer with internet access, you can go to one of the webcam static Centres over the summer, or when you arrive, and we'll help you to do it.

REQUIREMENTS FOR STUDENT ID CARD PHOTOS

You can upload your photo from any computer, phone or mobile device with Internet access.

We need a good quality passport style photo which must meet the following criteria:

1. The photo should be of you alone
2. Colour, clear with good contrast

Figure 1: Extract from the top Web hit for: *"How to get a student card in Wolverhampton?"* (source: `wlv.ac.uk`)

following the conventions used in the TexCoop tagger (see Tab. 1) to denote the abilities of a procedural tagger. While some of the HTML objects in the Webpage, such as title, headers and enumerations, are directly converted in their equivalent tags (`item`, `subtitle`), additional markup appears, such as warnings and prerequisites.

Table 1: TextCoop procedural markup (extract)

Label	Example
`title`	"Get your student ID card"
`subtitle`	"What you'll need"
`cond`	"if you are a UK student"
`objective`	"in order to get your ID"
`instr`	"Head to the Uni info service."
`prerequisite`	"You'll need 3 passport photos"
`warning`	"Format MUST be passport!"
`aim`	"to get good photos"
`advice`	"try the photobooth next to ..."

At this point, using a dialogue system to simply "read out" the above passage (even if split into their main components) would result in ineffective, close-to intonation free speech. Indeed, in order to provide instructions to the Natural Language Generator and Text-to-Speech modules of a dialogue system for verbalizing such text, dialogue-level markup must be added to the above procedural annotation.

In some cases, direct mapping rules can be devised to directly translate procedural markup into dialogue patterns. For instance, step-by-step instructions (`item`) contained in the `itemize` environment can be rendered as a sequence of *inform*

<subtitle> Applying for an ID card </subtitle>
<inst-compound>
When you receive a firm offer from the University,you can upload your photo for your student ID card, <warning> and you should do this as soon as you can. </warning>
</inst-compound>

<prerequisite> What you'll need
<itemize>
<item:1> Your student number, a seven-digit number which will be on your offer letter < /item:1>
<item:2> A digital photo that meets the requirements outlined below < /item:2>
<item:3> Access to a computer with Internet access to send your photo to the University using the Photo Upload facility.< /item:3>
</itemize></prerequisite>

<inst-compound> <cond> If you don't have a digital photo or a computer with internet access, </cond> ...

Figure 2: Procedural annotation of a Web page

<subtitle> Applying for an ID card </subtitle>
<inst-compound> When you receive a firm offer from the University, you can upload your photo for your student ID card, <warning> and you should do this < /prosody:emphasize> as soon as you can. < /prosody:emphasize> </warning> </inst-compound>

<prerequisite> What you'll need
<itemize>
<item:1> <dialog:inform-ack> Your student number, a seven-digit number which will be on your offer letter < /dialog:inform-ack> < /item:1>
<item:2> <dialog:inform-ack> A digital photo that meets the requirements outlined below < /dialog:inform-ack> < /item:2>
<item:3> <dialog:inform-ack> Access to a computer with Internet access to send your photo to the University using the Photo Upload facility. < /dialog:inform-ack> < /item:3>
</itemize> </prerequisite>

<inst-compound> <dialog:ask> <cond> If you don't have a digital photo or a computer with internet access,</cond> < /dialog:ask> ...

Figure 3: Dialog act and prosodic annotation of a Web page

dialogue acts, expecting acknowledgments (*ack*) from the user. In addition, conditions can be rendered as yes-no questions ("If you don't have a digital photo" becomes *ask(*digital photo*)*);

In other cases, such as verbalizing warnings and advice, specific salient words should be marked with prosodic information as to how to pronounce them. Specific lexical patters can be matched by rules to provide such annotations, such as "Remember" or "as soon as possible". Finally, part of the procedural annotation could be excluded from the dialog when redundant or implicit. For instance, titles (`title`) could be skipped or mentioned separately by the dialogue system (e.g. "Would you like to hear about how to *Get your student ID card*?").

Figure 3 illustrates the dialog act and prosodic annotation enriching the procedural one of Figure 2. Such generic markup can then me converted in a specific commercial voice markup languages, e.g. VXML or SALT, via simple rules.

5 Integrating Scenarios and QA

Besides improving access to procedures via direct interactions by spoken dialogue, it is often necessary to interact with the user to get more precise information about his query, so that the response can be accurate enough. Furthermore, a number of procedural questions do not get any direct response via Web queries. This is the case of type 2 questions, as introduced in Section 3. There are several reasons to this situation. First, a number of these questions are both complex and very specific. Next, most of them involve various forms of reasoning and of elaboration. Other questions require the integration of several simpler procedures, e.g. via concatenation. Finally, others require a substantial adaptation of existing procedures: adaptation to a different context, generalizations (e.g. knowing how to register in a university may lead to a generalization so that it is globally acceptable for other universities).

This is in particular the case for non-trivial itineraries. For example, looking on the Web for ways to go from Toulouse to Trento does not lead to any solution. Search engines return partial and often local information, e.g. description of Verona airport, train schedules going via Trento, etc. We need in this case to define a very generic scenario, which is a procedure, of type 'travel' and, for a given trip, to construct the details from simpler procedures or factual data available on the Web.

To overcome these limitations and to be able to offer a real QA service, we propose the following approach:

- Creating a general scenario, in our case for itinerary construction, involving dialogue to get necessary (departure/arrival location and dates, etc.) and optional (budget, comfort, etc.) information from the user.

- Including reasoning procedures and preferences related to transportation: e.g. it is preferable to fly above a certain distance or if there are obstacles (sea, mountains), or elaborate compromise between cost and transportation length. Itinerary construction also involves a planner, that operates over any kind of transportation means, paired with an optimizer. The planner should be flexible so that it can propose alternatives (e.g. train or renting a car, stops at different places) while the optimizer should take user preferences into account.

- Submitting queries to a search engine to get detailed information on precise points: flight schedules, airport transportation, bus routes, etc. Such queries are triggered by the different functions of the scenario to fill in information slots. From search engine results, it is necessary to process the text segments so that the correct information is found. This includes either getting precise data or selecting a text portion (e.g. that describes services, schedules, etc.).

- Summarizing the information and generating a response in natural language under the form of a procedure, possibly with schemas, maps, etc. and then producing a vocal output. As shown above, parts of this scenario may be vocal or multimedia. As in most natural language generation systems, this involves a planner that operates of various types of input data (text, words, structured sequences of the scenario) and a language generation component which, in this type of application, can be based on predefined word sequences and gaps to be filled in for the query at stake.

This approach has its roots in the frames and scripts of cognitive science and AI in the 70s (Schank and Abelson, 1977). However, in our case we include a QA component to get information and a planner to construct the itinerary based on the results of the queries which also outputs a procedure in natural language. In addition, the proposed approach supports cooperative dialogues and provides explanations to the user when there is no direct answer to his request.

6 Perspectives

We have proposed a model of procedural QA system conducting cooperative spoken dialogue with the user. Indeed, we argue that the advantages of spoken communication channel to address procedural QA are mainly twofold. On the one hand, procedural information can be returned to the user in a more efficient way compared to the textual format. On the other hand, cooperative dialogue allows the system to understand and refine the user's information needs and to account for the cases when information is not directly available on the Web.

Our proposed approach has currently only been validated through case studies and a long process is required in order to achieve spoken procedural QA. However, we believe that using existing resources to address procedural information, such as procedural taggers, as well as state-of-the art QA and spoken dialogue technology, fulfilling our objectives is a feasible task.

References

Y. Chen, M. Zhou, and S. Wang. 2006. Reranking answers from definitional QA using language models. In *Proc. ACL*.

E. Delpech and P. Saint-Dizier. 2008. Investigating the structure of procedural texts for answering how-to questions. In *Proc. LREC*.

N. Gupta, G. Tur, D. Hakkani-tur, G. Riccardi, S. Bangalore, M. Rahim, and M Gilbert. 2006. The AT&T spoken language understanding system. *IEEE transactions on speech and audio*, 14:213–222.

A. Moschitti, S. Quarteroni, R. Basili, and S. Manandhar. 2007. Exploiting syntactic and shallow semantic kernels for question/answer classification. In *Proc. ACL*.

C. Pechsiri, P. Sroison, and U. Janviriyasopa. 2008. Know-why extraction from textual data. In *Proc. KRAQ*.

R. C. Schank and R. P. Abelson. 1977. *Scripts, plans, goals, and understanding: An inquiry into human knowledge structures*. Erlbaum.

R. F. Simmons. 1965. Answering english questions by computer: a survey. *Comm. ACM*, 8(1):53–70.

D. Traum. 1996. Dialogue management in conversational agency: The TRAINS-93 dialogue manager. In *Proc. TWLT*, pages 1–11.

S. Verberne, L. Boves, N. Oostdijk, and P. Coppen. 2007. Evaluating discourse-based answer extraction for why-question answering. In *Proc. SIGIR*, pages 735–737.

E. M. Voorhees. 2003. Overview of TREC 2003. In *Proc. TREC*.

N. Webb and T. Strzalkowski, editors. 2006. *Proc. HLT-NAACL Workshop on Interactive Question Answering*.

L. Yin. 2006. A two-stage approach to retrieving answers for how-to questions. In *Proc. EACL (Student Session)*.

Author Index